# THE
# BLUFFER'S® GUIDE
# TO
# WHISKY

## DAVID MILSTED

◯
Oval Books

Published by Oval Books
335 Kennington Road
London SE11 4QE
United Kingdom

Telephone: +44 (0)20 7582 7123
Fax: +44 (0)20 7582 1022
E-mail: info@ovalbooks.com
Web site: www.ovalbooks.com

First published by Ravette Publishing, 1991

First published by Oval Books, 2000
Reprinted 2001, 2002

New Edition 2004


Series Editor – Anne Tauté

Cover designer – Rob Oliver
Cover image – © Doug Norman/Alamy
Printer – Cox & Wyman Ltd.
Producer – Oval Projects Ltd.

The Bluffer's® Guides series is based
on an original idea by Peter Wolfe.

ISBN-13: 978-1-903096-78-2
ISBN-10: 1-903096-78-2

# CONTENTS

# INTRODUCTION

The wonderful thing about whisky – apart, of course, from drinking it – is that it contains more bluffing elements than almost any other subject: even more than supply-side economics, and certainly more than wine. Wine can breed envy, discord and snobbery, whisky promotes fellowship, amiability and quiet, unassuming superiority.

Until quite recently whisky was a subject that tended to be monopolised by Scots, foreigners, and elderly gentlemen in Clubs. This made the whole area fairly barren ground for bluffers unless they were fortunate enough to find themselves in the company of North Americans with remote Highland ancestry. Such people have a pleasing habit of believing pretty well anything, up to and including the social benefits of the clan system and the romantic joys of kelp-gathering.

Things have changed. Whisky appreciation is an idea whose time has come. It will bring you into contact with much nicer people. Real people. Good people. Caring people... People like us.

Like all the best things in life, whisky is a fairly simple business that can easily be made to sound exclusive and impressive by a judicious application of the arcane and a liberal sprinkling of jargon. Knowledge of whisky, like love, is a matter of a basic theme made more enjoyable by an infinite number of variations. The really experienced may even find themselves able to combine the two, a thing real ale enthusiasts could never do.

Unlike that other great source of pleasure, however, whisky offers a field of activity in which a rapid turnover of partners (there are around 1,200 Scottish ones listed) is positively beneficial. As the poet A. E. Housman once put it: 'Malt does more than Milton can, to justify God's ways to man.'

In the last resort claim to be suffering from D.D.S. – Distillate Deficiency Syndrome. The essayist C. E. Montague was the first to analyse and codify this universal human affliction. 'I was born', he wrote, 'below par to the extent of two whiskies.' Which two is, of course, entirely up to you.

# THE BASICS

Whisky is a subject steeped in mystery and tradition. Since most of this is completely unknown to the average whisky drinker, the amount of hard work required on your part is reassuringly small.

There are two eternal truths about whisky:

1. No two whiskies are alike.

2. Ninety nine per cent of whisky drinkers cannot tell the difference until it is revealed to them.

If you keep pointing out number 1 while bearing number 2 in mind, you cannot go wrong.

The dictionary defines whisky as: 'Spirit distilled from malted barley, other grains, etc.; kind of light gig or chaise' which is precise, lucid, incontrovertible and most unhelpful, but of course ideal for whisky bluffers because it provides practically unlimited scope for improvisation.

The word 'whisky' is derived from the Gaelic 'uisge beatha' (pronounced 'ooshki baah') meaning 'water of life'. The ancient Romans called their alcohol 'aqua vitae', which sounds remarkably similar, if you make the effort.

The avatar of whiskies is *Ferintosh*, an incredibly ancient, semi-apocryphal liquor, drunk by Methusela to celebrate his 900th year. "The real *Ferintosh*" is thus the ultimate accolade but should only be applied to something you drank once, long ago. It was last made, duty-free, by the Forbes family of Culloden, and the ending of this civilised arrangement towards the close of the 18th century caused Robert Burns (who was once employed as an exciseman, though he is now thought of as having been on the other end of the whisky process, as it were) to write: 'O Ferintosh, o sadly lost!' Like much of Burns' best poetry, this sounds better if you've had a whisky or two.

# Varieties

There are four of these to get to grips with – Malt whisky, Grain whisky, Blended whisky, and Others.

## Malt Whisky

**Scottish Malt** whisky should always be called 'malt' and thought of as the Real Stuff. Successful malt-bluffing involves the only remotely hard work you have to do, which is to memorise a few key words to describe the things that are done to make it. These are set out in ravishing detail later on (see Glossary: The Process).

Meanwhile, all you need to remember is that it is made entirely from barley, using a **pot-still**. This is important. Malt whisky distilling is a beautifully simple process, and anyone with a reasonably large, plumbed-in potting shed could do it – were it not for spoilsports like Customs and Excise whose job it is to ensure that the simple, wholesome pleasures of life cost 75% more per bottle than they need to.

**Irish Malt** whiskey is made in much the same way as the Real Stuff, except that it is distilled three times instead of two. This makes it smoother and rounder (or, if you prefer, blander) than Scottish malt, and could be said to account for the higher price per bottle.

Point out that Irish whiskey is spelled differently from Scottish whisky because the ancient Scots (who were originally Irish) spoke a different sort of Gaelic to the ancient Irish (who were originally Hungarian). In fact, Scottish whisky was also spelled this way up to around the time of the 1916 Easter Rebellion.

Irish whiskey tastes sweeter because no peat is used to kiln the malt; this is odd for a country that has virtually more bog per hectare than anywhere else on the planet and possibly has something to do with the fact that most Irish peat ends up in bags in garden centres.

Irish whiskey can also be made with potatoes and is called poteen. This is:

a) illegal, and

b) not what you might call an altogether edifying experience.

## Grain Whisky

Grain whisky is made from maize (as are cornflakes) which is ground up and mixed with a little malted barley (usually in a ratio of 9:1). Fermentation then takes place before distillation in a **patent still** (or Coffey still, named after the cunning profiteer who invented it) to emerge as 'silent spirit' – an alcoholic substance that may be blended as Scotch whisky or further refined to make gin or vodka.

## Blended Whisky

A mixture of malt whisky and grain whisky, of which more later.

# Others

## Bourbon

A whisky made in North America from a mixture of maize and wheat or barley in an attempt to compensate for the lack of bens, glens, bogs, midges, rain and lost causes so essential to the making of the Real Stuff. It is named after Aristophanes Q. Bourbon III, the Kentucky inventor of the chocolate sandwich biscuit.

## Sour Mash

Another transatlantic ex-colonial imitation, so called because of the addition of acetic acid to the cereal grains in order to chivvy along the fermentation process. Also known as 'sippin' whisky', presumably because only an idiot would risk taking a whole mouthful. It may be that idiots are especially thick on the ground in Tennessee, but it is probably wiser not to speculate.

## Japanese Whisky

A Scots distiller said of Japanese whisky: 'If you drank it all day and all night you might end up thinking it was like Scotch whisky. But by then you might be dead.'

Japan's efforts to make the water of life range from importing bulk malt whisky and mixing it with neutral spirit, to producing an instant powdered whisky (just add instant soda). On the other hand,

Japan has become a substantial investor in the malt whisky industry. This is a sobering thought – enough to make you rush out and buy a case or two of the Real Stuff.

## Liqueur Whisky

There is considerable debate as to whether 'liqueur whiskies' like *Drambuie* and *Glayva* ought to be regarded as whiskies at all, and we suggest you prolong discussions until the bottle in question has been squeezed dry.

In favour of classing them as whiskies is the fact that they all have varying amounts of whisky in them, but then, so does whisky-mac (a mixture of whisky and ginger wine). On the other hand, they all contain unforgivable things like herbs, honey, and fruit, and ought therefore to belong firmly in the 'sticky' class, along with those dark chocolates with the centres that taste of expensive cough linctus. It can be a fascinating post-prandial debate, particularly if someone else is buying.

Note that '*Drambuie*' derives from the Gaelic for 'yellow drink', rather than 'an dram buidheach' – 'the drink that satisfies'. Scotland is full of hills called Ben Buie and lochs called Loch Buie, and none of them is supposed to be satisfying.

The secret recipe for *Drambuie* is alleged to have been given to a Captain MacKinnon of Skye by Charles Edward Stewart as a thankyou for not betraying him to the English. Bonnie Prince Charlie then went to Rome and drank himself to death – not, you should hasten to add, on whisky.

11

# BLENDED WHISKY

Blended whisky, a mixture of malt whisky and grain whisky, is the drink most people think of as being 'whisky' or 'Scotch' (a word that must never be used on its own).

The practice of blending took off in the second half of the 19th century – so it has had plenty of time to reach the summit of perfection where art meets science. The first marketed blend was launched in 1853. Called *Usher's Old Vatted Glenlivet*, it was remarkable for being neither old nor, for the most part, *Glenlivet*. Much has changed since then, and the practice of blending is now a highly skilled and tightly regulated business.

Most of the malt whiskies used for blending are four years old, though one or two blends (e.g., *Mackinlays*) use five and others, such as *Bell's 8-year-old*, make a virtue of even greater age. Maturer malt makes a better blend. The most affordable ones use malt matured for the legal minimum of three.

All blended Scotch whiskies, then, contain a proportion of the Real Stuff. The question is how much, and which? Luckily this is a question which, for 99% of all available blends, cannot be answered. Be sure to take full advantage of this mystery.

## What's in It?

You would be better advised to try cracking the formula of Coca-Cola, than attempt to discover what has gone into a bottle of your usual brand of blended whisky. Producers of blended whisky will tell you that their fine produce is the result of exhaustive testing (by nose rather than mouth) of as many as 50 different sorts of malt and grain spirit, and that they dare not, for fear of precipitating the Apocalypse, reveal its mysteries. You might reply – as an ordinary mortal, rather than a bluffer – that a listing on the label of, say, the five principal malts would do no harm and be of interest to the consumer. But you'd be wasting your breath; blenders seem to be immune even to European Union legislation on product labelling.

The points to bear in mind are:

1. The average blended brand will contain 20-39% malt whisky, the dearer ones 40-50%, and many economy blends as little as 10%.

2. Two blended whiskies which do declare themselves, and which you, of course, will keep very quiet about about are:

   *Old Highland Blend* (Eldridge, Pope & Co., Dorset). Principal malts are *Glenfarclas, Glenfiddich, Glen Grant* and *Glenrothes-Glenlivet*.

   *Queen's Liqueur* (W.G. McFadden & Co., Giffnock). 50% malt whisky, viz: *Glen Grant* and *The Glenlivet*.

The serious bluffer will always have a decanter of one of these handy.

Secrecy, then, gives you plenty of room for manoeuvre. One straightforward bluff is to name:

   (a) your favourite malt, and
   (b) your preferred blend,

and insist that (b) contains a significant amount of (a). Unless the person you are talking to happens to be the distiller of (a) or the blender of (b) there is no way of being caught out.

Alternatively, learn (and then destroy) the following list of blends, together with their distinctive malt whisky constituents, or 'fillings' as blenders call them:

| | |
|---|---|
| *Ballantine's* | — Inverleven (Lowland), |
| | — Miltonduff (Speyside) and |
| | — Scapa (Orkney) |
| *Bell's* | — Blair Athol (Perthshire) |
| *Bell's 8-year-old* | — Dufftown (Speyside) |
| *Clan Campbell* | — Aberlour (Speyside) |
| *Crawford's 3- and 5-Star* | — Benrinnes (Speyside) |
| *Dewar's White Label* | — Aberfeldy (Perthshire) |
| *Famous Grouse* | — Bunnahabhainn (Islay), |
| | Tamdhu (Speyside) and |
| | Highland Park (Orkney) |
| *Grant's* | — Balvenie (Speyside) and |
| | Glenfiddich (Speyside) |
| *John Barr* | — Mortlach (Speyside) |
| *Johnny Walker* | — Cardhu (Speyside) |
| *Old Parr* | — Glendullan (Speyside) and |
| | Cragganmore (Speyside) |
| *Stewart's Cream of the Barley* | — Clencadam (Northern) |
| *White Horse* | — Lagavulin (Islay) and |
| | Glen Elgin (Speyside) |

Your claim to be able to detect these ingredients can be backed up by referring to the distinguishing characteristics of the malt whisky region in question (see Regions). If challenged, tap your nose meaningfully and say, "It's all in here. Once nosed, always recognised." This is unanswerable, and has a wonderfully irritating effect.

14

# De Luxe or Premium Blends

Generally, a de luxe blend ought to justify its higher price by having more malt in it (at least 50%) and being older (eight years-old or more) than the standard fare. Pot-distilling takes longer and maize is about half the price of barley, so the higher price of de luxe whisky can be justified if there is appreciably more malt in the blend. But it can be quite a big 'if'.

All maturer, maltier blends will be more expensive, but not all the more expensive blends are necessarily maturer or maltier. And blenders who give this information away are rarer than hens' teeth. *Bell's Islander* contains Islay malts (as its name implies); otherwise, you are pretty well on your own.

An excellent point to make is that not all malt whiskies blend well together; a de luxe blend may contain (say) 60% malt whiskies and have been aged for ten years but this does not mean it will be good to drink if the malts used are not the sort that 'marry' well: thus one can always dismiss someone else's de luxe blend as 'a disastrous misalliance'.

A disappointing de luxe might be positively 'non-consanguineous', or even 'morganatic'. This is a good ploy for those who would rather not admit to being hard up.

Alternatively – and especially if bluffing in the company of socialists, Greens, hunt saboteurs and so forth – point out that one of the better-known blends, *Islay Mist*, was originally concocted in honour of the coming-of-age of the man who went on to become President of the British Field Sports Association and Britain's last created hereditary baron. This could be a pretty good reason for letting someone else buy it.

## Super De Luxe Blends

These are around 20 years old, contain about 75% malt, and will return very little change from a £50 note. "You could buy two bottles of a first-class unadulterated malt for the price of a bottle of this," you observe, as you hold out your glass for a refill. "Still, just to keep you company ..."

## Supermarket Blends

What few of us will admit to drinking, these are likely to be three years old (just) and no more than 15% malt. However, since most of us do buy them, we recommend they be decanted and passed off as having been blended 'to your taste' by one of your contacts north of the Highland Line (a mythical but useful barrier in this case). *De gustibus non est disputandum\**, as they say in Drumnadrochit.

Choose supermarket 'own-brand' in preference to cheaper labels with names like *'Hoots Mon!'* or *'Big Yin'*: supermarket chains have a reputation to defend. Read the label carefully and, if it says '37.5 alcohol/65° proof', put the bottle back on the shelf with a curl of the lip and a barely suppressed hiss. Under-proofing may be fine for gin (you just drink more gin or add less tonic) but drinking under-proof whisky is only for the truly desperate, i.e., when there is nothing else left on the shelf.

* 'There's no accounting for taste', but it sounds more profound in Latin.

# Single Grain Whisky

Rarely available – *Cameron Brig* and *The Invergordorn* are two you can mention – single grain whiskies are 100% silent spirit, that is to say, the product of a patent still and containing no malt whisky at all. Amazing but true: absolutely none whatsoever. You should describe its flavour as distinctive (naturally) while noting that the professionals all agree on its 'rather peculiar medicinal flavour', though they don't actually say which peculiar medicine they have in mind.

# Miniatures

Many tourists will, when deprived of any other sort of item, buy miniature bottles of whisky, some of which are brands that have no existence in any other sort of container. Bluffers should have no truck with them, except when they are offered free by distillery managers. Point out that collecting miniature whiskies is a singularly senseless hobby, since they are worthless if you open them, and pointless if you don't. Their cost prices the contents at around £1 a sip, which is absurd by any standards.

You may, however, evince a passing fondness for the following miniatures of Scotch whisky, bourbon and Canadian rye: *Old Taylor, Old Forester, Cairngorm, Four Roses, Dimple Haig, Hiram Walker, Harper's, Kentucky Tavern, Red Label, Dunosdale Cream, Lord Calvert, George IV, Queen Anne, Highland Queen, Vat 69, Standfast* and *Old Argyll*. These were all the pieces drunk during the famous game of draughts between Wormold and Captain Segura in Graham Greene's *Our Man in Havana*.

# Name Your Bluff

Malt whiskies tend to take their brand names from their distilleries; most blended whiskies, on the other hand, appear to have been christened by the sort of people who go on to call their retirement bungalows 'Erzanmine'.

## Common Names

In their unrelenting quest for a name that sounds vaguely Scottish and romantic, purveyors often seem to have got stuck in a misty Caledonian groove, for example:

**Black** – The first name of 22 whiskies, presumably inspired by the Black Watch, the black grouse, Black Donald of the Isles, the Black Knight of Lorne, the Black Acts, blackface sheep, etc. Known to the politically correct as 'without-milk'. *Black & White* whisky is enjoyed by British Members of Parliament under a House of Commons label.

**Bonnie** – First name of half a dozen deservedly unheard-of brands which, you will maintain, are drunk only by people who display nodding Loch Ness Monsters in their rear car windows.

**Clan** – First name of 14 whiskies, including *Clan Campbell* (owned by Pernod), *Clan House* (The Rum Co. Ltd. of Basle), and *Clan Munro* (the General Beverage Corp. of Luxembourg, better known as Martini-Rossi).

18

**Glen** – The prefix of 127 whiskies, not counting strength or age variations of the same brand. There is even one called *Glenmillar*. Claim to be on a lifetime's quest to track down and sample all 127 including *Glenkinchie*, the last single malt in the Lothians. It is extraordinary how eager people can be to help with this sort of ludicrous project.

**Gold** or **Golden** – The first name of 27 whiskies, six of them called *Gold Label*. *Fleischsmann's Golden Glen* is the highly improbable name of a blended whisky shipped from Scotland in bulk and bottled in the United States.

**Highland** – The first name of 39 whiskies. *Highland Queen* (named after the one who lost her head) was the first whisky ever to be marketed in Egypt, and is rumoured to contain more malt than most.

**King** or **King's** – The first name of 44 whiskies including *King Size*, *King Dick*, *King Alfred* (cakes added to the peat) and *King of Kings*. Most of Scotland's kings were called Robert, James or Alexander, but no whisky is named after Alexander and *MacBeth* is no longer available. However, some rather unlikely English monarchs are represented by the splendid firm of Henry Stenham & Co., whose blends include: *King Edgar, King Edmund II, King John, King Henry VII* and *Old Arthur*. Stenham's offers all its 35 whiskies in a choice of ages (3, 5, 8, 10 and 12-years-old) and bottle shapes, which is good fun.

**Old** – The first name of 85 whiskies (101 if you count 'Auld') some of which are very silly (see Silly names). Look out for *Old Fettercairn* single malt: it is distilled by a firm founded by Mr. Gladstone's father, which probably explains his son's knowledge of the angel's share and sympathy for the respectable drinking classes.

**Queen** or **Queen's** – The first name of 22 whiskies, including *Queen's Liqueur* and two *Queen Elizabeths*. Avoid Queen Margot (in some 'continental' supermarkets) unless you actually enjoy headaches.

**Royal** – The first name of 62 whiskies, most of which are exported to republics. None of them is by appointment to HM the Queen.

Watch out for the frequent use of 'rare' and 'special' in brand names. Their meaning can be defined as:
(a) expensive
(b) ordinary, or
(c) both.

## Silly Names

There is no need to invent your own when you can choose from the following real ones:

*Blue Hanger, Gee Gee, Glen Tosh, Grog Blossom, Kilt Castle, Mac King Gay Ghost, Monster's Choice, Old Age, Old Barrister, Old Cobblers, Old Crypt, Old Fellah, Old Label, Pheasant Plucker, Pig's Nose, Plus Fours, Queen Size, Red Capsule, Red Tape, Regal Butt, Royal Pheasant, Scotch Pillar, Sheep Dip, Tee Tee, Twinkle, Upstairs, Wat Tyler* and *Wham's Dram*.

Suggest that the silliest ones of all are derived from the names of fishing flies.

## Phoney Names

Foreign brands of so-called 'Scotch whisky' can be made by mixing small quantities of exported malt with large quantities of home-made heaven-knows-what and selling them under authentic-sounding names, such as *Captain Jock* (Greece) and *Loch Ness Scotch Whisky* (Italy)\*, both of which have been suppressed following legal action.

All good bluffers should claim to have sampled some of the following, spotted overseas:

*Duck Scot* (Brazil)
*Gaylord* (Germany)
*Old Windjammer* (Italy)
*Camerone Cream of the Glen* (Malawi)
*Kilt* (Spain)
*King Victoria* (Japan)
*Auld Piss* (Ecuador).

# Characteristics

Blended whiskies have their own characteristics all of which are contributed by the malt whiskies that are used to make them. So a successful blended whisky bluff relies on a knowledge of the Bluffing Elements (see next section) of malt whisky, even if you never drink it – superficiality in depth being the secret of a killer bluff.

---

\* Italy is the world's biggest importer of bottled malt whisky. No-one knows why. (Italians say the reason is simple: they like the best.)

# MALT WHISKY

As well as being, on its own, the noblest drink on earth, malt whisky (as you will know if you've been paying attention) finds its way, in varying quantities, into every bottle of blended Scotch whisky, however cheap and cheerful. Without it, Britain's laughably misnamed balance of payments would look a whole lot worse. Yet it is the product of fewer than a hundred working distilleries north of Hadrian's Wall.

Malt accounts for a substantial portion of the lore, mystique and hagiography of whisky (not to mention the bosh, bunkum and balderdash), and your pretence to a good grounding in its various elements, types and regions will thus form an essential part of any successful attempt to kid, beguile, hoodwink, hoax, humbug or otherwise hornswoggle innocent bystanders in your vicinity.

## The Bluffing Elements

All the kilning, malting, brewing, distilling and casking required in the making of malt (see Glossary) provides a wealth of material for the meretriciously educated bluffer.

Begin with just one element of this process and, when you have proved your ability, proceed to two or more in combination. But take care not to end up contradicting yourself by (for example) demonstrating that the water used to distil your whisky makes it ethereally pure and fragrant, while at the same time maintaining that the peat used to malt the barley contributes to its sooty pungency. Your best plan, should you see such a blatant self-contradiction looming, is to proclaim it a "manifest synthesis".

Picture yourself dram in hand and eager to say something memorable about it. "Ah," you begin, "now what we have here is very interesting, you see, because of the ... (water, barley, peat, yeast, cask colour or pot-still) ..." as follows:


# Water

As one of the principal variables of whisky, water should enable you to anatomise the contents of your glass in terms that leave the average wine enthusiast eating your dust.

Water is one of the reasons why the Real Stuff cannot be made outside Scotland, the assumption being that Scottish water is pure and clean, and soft – the sort of water that foams if you wave a bar of soap over it. This is most true of the Highlands, which are not blighted by factories, chemical waste dumps, spin doctors and so forth.

Enthuse about its unique 'Highland qualities', that is to say ready-infused with mystic trace elements of peat, granite, heather, midge, tweed, damp and Roman Ninth Legion.

Its origin is as important in the production of Speyside malts, for instance, as hard Trent water is in the brewing of Burton Ale, and it cannot be imitated. Refer to variables of:

1. **Supply** – Does it come from a spring, a burn, a river, or a loch? Is it the crystal-clear stuff contained in bottles, or the high-fibre variety that stains enamel baths brown in Ardnamurchan?

**2. Season** – What was the weather like when it was made? The biochemical profile of Scottish water may be completely altered by a period of heavy rain or (slightly less common) a heatwave. This can cause wide variation between two batches of whisky from the same distillery; it is therefore the main source of impressive-sounding intelligence for **single-cask** (q.v.) malt, and the rough equivalent of a wine expert's 'late vintage' ploy.

Tell the tale of two rare single malt whiskies *Glen Mhor* and *Glen Albyn* – the produce of two distilleries which were once situated a few hundred yards apart on the banks of the River Ness. Both, according to reliable authority, used the same malt, peat, yeast, size and type of still and cask: each was matured for the same period. Yet the difference in taste between the two is unmistakable. The only thing that could possibly account for this is the water: each drew its supply from a different source in the river. This, at any rate, was the story of their late proprietor, and if he was prepared to stick to it, you can too.

# Barley

Most distillers will insist that the source and type of their barley has no influence on the taste or quality of their product; this is because most distillers these days have very little control over where their barley comes from, or what sort it is.

Where once Scotland's distilleries were self-sufficient in grain, often grown in their own fields, now it might as easily come from Ireland, England, Canada, the United States or even Australia. Point out that origin and type of grain is a significant and variable factor. So, you could try saying: "I fear this has been made with barley from…" [insert a nation from the list above]. Then drink it anyway, just to be sociable.

If your drink tastes 'bready', blame overenthusiasm in the grinding mill; if you find it tends to cauterise your nostrils before your lips can get to it, make a passing reference to 'original moisture', the moisture content of the barley after it has been malted – usually around 3% but can be lower, as in whiskies that make you thirsty. This is another thing that distilleries who buy their grain ready-malted cannot properly control.

Alternatively, mutter something about being able to detect a hint of decayed mouse droppings and suggest that the barley could not have been 'properly dressed'. With a bit of luck you may be allowed the rest of the bottle all to yourself.

# Peat

Traditional distilleries kiln their malt over a peat furnace; modern ones puff peat smoke through it after kilning. Either way, peat is a crucial element. (Never call Irish whiskey 'peaty', remember, because the Irish don't use it.)

The splendid thing about peat is that it is very variable. Since it is formed from compressed layers of dead vegetation, it takes its 'character' – chemical composition, mass, texture, aroma when burnt and so forth – from the nature of its changing environment, from prehistoric times right up to the day it was cut. Peat cut near the surface is porous, spongy, pale and rooty; the deeper you go, the denser and darker and more ancient it gets.

All this ought to give you plenty of scope for suggesting that the particular and unmistakable 'nose', flavour, texture or **finish** of what you are drinking can be accounted for by the sheep pellets/seaweed/bog oak/giant elk/neolithic remains contained in the peat used in its manufacture. "A hint of iodine on the tongue," you will pronounce "is the unmistakable sign of a coastal distillery" (say Islay, Orkney or Caithness to be on the safe side). All you have to do is invent the evidence to match your conclusion.

As a general rule, you should insist that only malt whisky from a distillery that still cuts its own peat to kiln its own malt can count as the Real Stuff. But take care: you may find yourself championing one that cuts its peat on a site of special scientific interest inhabited by the Lesser Spotted Bog-Warbler and defended by hordes of environmentally-conscious television personalities.

If you need a clincher for your peat-bluff, observe that peat smoke contains organic ring compounds with double carbon-carbon bonds – a sure-fire sign of pungency. Few things are more effective than a strategically-deployed scientific fact.


# Yeast

"Ah," you murmur as you take another life-enhancing slurp of your host's supply, "the perfect zymurgy". (This is what happens when you ferment things – such as wort, in a distillery – with yeast.)

Yeast is a living organism (though whether it is an animal is the subject of heated debate among vegans) and it feeds on sugar to produce alcohol, a product which eventually kills it.

What you need to impress upon others is that:

a) distilleries use more than one type of yeast, and
b) often these carefully selected yeasts have been used once already, in brewing beer.

A quick search through records at Companies House has revealed to you the relationship between (for instance) *McEwan's Export Ale* and *Isle of Jura* malt, or *Guinness Extra Stout* and *Dewar's*.

Yeast, you will insist, makes an essential contribution to the distinctive quality of a whisky – quite what that is, is entirely up to you. We recommend frequent use of the phrase 'almost intangible' for this one.

## Pot-stills

The malt still, known as a pot-still, is one of the glories of creation. Made of gleaming, burnished copper its voluptuous belly curves gracefully upwards in one poignant swoop of beaten metal and then declines, with consummate, breathtaking artistry in a thrilling swan's-neck dive before descending into the hidden mysteries of the condenser.

The important thing to remember about pot-stills is that no two are exactly alike, a fact that puts them firmly in the 'bluffing variants' category. Some are squat onion-shaped affairs; others are the traditional pear shape; still others look like inverted tulip glasses. Each has its own special way of condensing the compounds in whisky. There are up to 800 known compounds and how they relate to each other and how they affect the flavour has never been established. The only way to find out, of course, is through a lifetime's dedicated hard sampling.

Call science to your aid by remarking that the composition (always copper) and surface configuration of a pot-still determine the manner in which the chemical reactions take place. It is for this reason that old stills are supposedly replaced with new ones which are an exact replica of the original. This should lead you neatly to the Famous Dented Still Story, which you may safely apply to any distillery you choose to mention and use to justify your choice of something expensive when it's someone else's turn to pay.

## The Famous Dented Still Story

Once upon a time, in a distillery in Scotland, a stillman had an unfortunate accident, the exact circumstances of which are not clear, but the consequence of which was that the still sustained a severe dent.

Everyone held their breath until the first produce of the violated still was sampled, but the whisky was better than ever, and over the succeeding decades the still continued to pour forth a spirit sustaining alike to body and soul. In fact, so successful was the dented still and so distinctive its yielded essence that when it was worn out and needed to be replaced, an identical dent was deliberately rendered in the replacement. In this way, the consistency of the product was assured and maintained.

When telling this story as an explanation of why Brand X is your favourite single malt you need not fear that your audience will make the pilgrimage to the distillery to find out if you're bluffing – and even if they do, the odds are they will find that you are not.

An additional still-bluff concerns **pot ale** – the gungy stuff left behind after the first distillation. In many stills that are fired from below (as opposed to being steam-heated) the gunge can get itself baked on to the bottom of the still and give that particular run of spirit a charcoaly-treacly flavour. To prevent this, the still is fitted inside with a large, slow-motion whisk called a **rummager**.

"Ah-hah," you rumble, rolling the golden blood of Scotia around your mouth before letting it slip sensuously down your throat, "this has all the hallmarks of being cut from an imperfectly rummaged run." In order to explain this fully, of course, you will need to sample at least one more large dram.

## Cask (Bluffese for 'barrel')

All whisky must mature for a minimum of three years in casks (unlike wine, it does not benefit from being kept in a bottle) and all casks must be made of oak. Zealots are fond of calling them 'oaken', a word much favoured by manufacturers who also put 'auld' on the label.

The three-year period for whisky was imposed after exhaustive surveys of the Scottish climate, which tends towards the cooler, damper end of the meteorological spectrum (especially in the Northern Isles). Faster-maturing whisky will thus be one of the compensations of the latter stages of the Greenhouse Effect. At the beginning of the 20th century, *Australian Bonded Grand Liqueur*, a product of Wm Teacher & Sons, was sent in casks to Australia in the belief that the ozone would enhance the maturing process, and Australians were hardly likely to notice if it didn't. Australia got its own back some years later by exporting Rupert Murdoch and *Neighbours*.

Many distilleries, especially those owned by a mega-consortium, have no control over their supply of casks and no idea what sort they are going to get next. This can have a dramatic effect on the colour of the branded product (to say nothing of the texture, bouquet or palate) – and, of course, gives you an ideal opening for explaining why your dram of Ben Thingy is lighter/darker/oilier/rounder/sharper than the last one you had.

The flavour of whisky depends partly on its reaction with the components of wood. These are cellulose, hemicellulose, lignin and a host of volatile oils, acids, sugars, steroids, tannins, pigments and inorganic compounds (they have never succeeded in counting them all) providing free rein for the imaginative, uninhibited bluffer, especially if you have had a couple.

About 2% of the maturing whisky is lost by evaporation: this is known as the angels' share and is the cause of much deep breathing in bonded warehouses. In the 19th century, Mr. Gladstone generously altered the excise duty on whisky to take account of this loss. Lloyd-George, on the other hand, raised whisky duty by 39% in 1909, tried to nationalise the Scottish distilleries in 1915, closed down all the pot-stills in 1917 and, a year later, doubled the whisky duty. But then, he was not only a Temperance man, he was also Welsh. A more whisky-friendly politician was Winston Churchill who, in 1945, ensured that supplies of barley went to the distillers instead of being frittered away on such post-war essentials as food.

# Colour

Whisky begins its life as a colourless spirit and gains its hue in one of four ways – you will of course claim to distinguish between them – by being matured in:

1. Old oak casks previously used for the storage of sherry, particularly oloroso and fino. This is the traditional, time-honoured, craft-hallowed way, now hardly done any more.

   Claim to be drinking sherrified whisky if you can tell from the resonantly amber-clear look and tell-tale vinous grace-notes on the palate, or if you happen to know it's *The Macallan*.

2. Spit-new oak casks that have had their insides briefly set on fire. Little specks of charcoal in your glass are a dead giveaway for this method.

3. Casks which have been smeared with 'pajarette', a brownish treacly stuff made from evaporated grape juice. Declare that this makes the whisky brownish, treacly, etc.

4. Casks painted with caramel. Caramel is known to induce cancer in Californian rats; on the other hand, whisky probably cures them. It is a risk worth taking, on the whole.

Not surprisingly, only the diminishing band of category 1 whiskies will own up to the method used, though most 'All About Scotch Whisky' leaflets would have us believe that it is universal.

You might try remarking that a little gravy browning in one's dram is nothing compared with all the food dyes and agrochemicals that go into the average bottle of vin rouge.

Alternatively, venture to recommend white whisky. Matured without benefit of sherry cask, pajarette or caramel but otherwise indistinguishable from ordinary whisky, white whisky has never really caught on, despite being marketed at about a pound a bottle less. It is inadvisable to admit an affection for it for no other reason than that, like vodka, it can be swigged from a glass without arousing suspicion. This is a secret better kept to yourself.


# The Payoff

Sooner or later, some know-all is going to interrupt you and announce that all this stuff about peat, water, yeast, oak and copper bellies is nothing more than tales devised by the distillers to prop up the mystique of their product and keep their prices high. Your bluff, in other words, will be called.

Here we suggest you use the sad (but encouraging) story of the Alko Company, of Finland.


## The Alko Story

Alko is the name of the Finnish state-owned company that spent much the best part of a decade trying to distil a 'Scotch whisky' of its own in an effort to make the 24-hour winter evenings more bearable. In their attempt to do so, boffins succeeded in isolating 400 chemical compounds (out of the 800 or so available) which contribute to the flavour, of which no less than 44 turn out to be from the oak used for the casks.

Using pot-stills specially made to imitate Speyside's finest, and yeast imported from Scotland, they at last succeeded in producing some bottles of Bonnie Helsinki Special Reserve Scottish-Type Whisky Drink. Understandably, Lalli Nykänen, head of the project, is on record as preferring to drink 12-year-old *Glenlivet*.

The Alko story touches on all the bluffing elements of your subject, and you should tell it whenever the bluff gets tough. It is a salutary reminder of what happens to people who do not take bluffers seriously.

# Types of Malt

Malt whisky can be bought in three types; these are – in descending order of affordability – vatted malt, single malt and single-cask malt.

## Vatted Malt

This is expensive. It usually comes with an ornate label, rich in scrolls and curlicues. A bottle of vatted malt contains malt whiskies from two or more distilleries – as opposed to a single malt, which is the unique product of one. The malts used are, you may safely say, often selected out of a suspicion that they are not quite good enough to make it on their own – though of course you must add (before you get sued) that some vatted malts are 'very good indeed'. Some people say they are bland, characterless and off-puttingly syrupy in flavour, but that is just their opinion.

What is lacking in a bottle of this sort is very often more than compensated for by adjectival overload on the label, where such words as 'fine', 'Royal', 'reserve', 'extra special', 'old', and even 'auld' proliferate. Unfortunately, it is often quite hard to find the bit where they tell you it's a mixture. What you need to look for is the missing word – 'single' or 'unblended' – and the missing information: the name and address of the distillery. Do not be misled by the word 'pure' – you wouldn't really expect it to have industrial effluent in it, after all.

Note that the age on the label must by law apply to the youngest whisky in the mixture, so a bottle of eight-year-old vatted malt will contain whiskies that are, ooh, eight years and a fortnight old, at least.

## Single Malt

This is even more expensive. There are over a hundred single malt whiskies, of various ages and strengths, around 10% of which are widely promoted; the full range is available at one of the meccas of malt, such as Gordon & MacPhail's of Elgin or Mulroy's of Old Compton Street, London.

Malts come in a bewildering variety of ages (8, 10, 12, 15, 20, 25 and even, though this is pushing it a bit, 50 years) and proof strengths (70°, 75°, 80° and 100°). To be on the safe side, claim to enjoy best a brand which has been matured for 12 years and bottled at a proof strength of 80°: it is the sort that professional zealots usually go for. Anything less than this, you maintain, is best kept for people who need to be impressed, such as your bank manager.

Pick a more-or-less unheard of name – *Ben Nevis, Old Pulteney, MacPhail's, Glen Scotia, Glenturret, Glenesk, Scapa, Caperdonich, Cragganmore* – and insist that it is the only one worth drinking. Explain why by lavish association of peat, pot-stills and water.

Alternatively, simply say, "Oh, it has to be a Glenlivet" – but not *The Glenlivet* – "for me, every time." This will open up whole new bluffing vistas (see Glenlivet).

Another virtually impregnable pose is to announce that the only malt whisky you would be prepared to spend your hard-won earnings on is one which comes from a distillery that carries out every single process – from barley-steeping to cooperage – on the premises, using time-honoured methods dating back to the days of the Industrial Revolution. There are not many that do this; indeed, as many Islay distilleries do it as in the whole of the rest of Scotland.

As there are (at present) around 120 distilleries in the rest of Scotland and seven in Islay, the chances are that your companion's choice of tipple will not be the real Real Stuff. You will, of course, then proceed to reveal why it isn't, while drinking as many samples as you can get away with in order to illustrate your exegesis.

Keep this going until you have convinced your listener that single malt whisky is the sine qua non of the distiller's art. It isn't, however; this distinction belongs to:

## Single-Cask Malt

Utterly pocket-crippling. In real life, supplies of this spirit are only available to the likes of merchant bankers, Premiership footballers, senior government advisers, EU commissioners, judges, chat-show hosts, and dodgy Russian businessmen, but this shouldn't prevent you pretending to have a secret source of supply. We can all dream.

Single malt is the produce of a single distillery – but of several distillations, blended together in an effort to ensure product consistency. The phrase '10-year-old malt' can cover up to twelve months' production from a number of stills. A single-cask malt, on the other hand, is the result of only *one* distillation, its unique character stamped on it by all the variable elements in their most extreme form. It is ferociously expensive, even if you can get hold of it, which, on the whole, you can't. But don't let this put you off; if you are looking for a sure-fire way of winning your spurs as a whisky advocate, this is it.

# The Ultimate Bluff

Having first assured total privacy, take an empty whisky bottle from which you have removed the label (make sure the glass is not embossed with the trade mark of whatever it contained previously) and fill to about two-thirds (more would be vulgar) with an ordinary malt or, if you haven't been able to raise a mortgage to buy one, one of the paler (hence more interesting-looking) blends – *J&B Rare* or *Cutty Sark* will do nicely.

Invite your guest to sit down while you produce the bottle and pace the room – premier cru bluffing, like porridge-eating, is best done this way – as you prepare your prey with a long story about how you have an understanding with the distillery (choose one of the obscure ones, just in case) which ensures that your supply is distilled only from barley grown by the Findhorn Community, kilned with peat laid down during the Early Bronze Age and cut from a croft adjoining a raised beach, then steeped in water drawn immediately after a light spring shower with a West-South-Westerly breeze; fermented with a yeast used previously for the brewing of Fowler's Wee Heavy* and vaporised in the pot-still dented by Alasdair 'Thumbs' MacFadyen during the Disruption of 1843; matured in oak casks which formerly stored a Golden Oloroso made only by Jesuit Fathers in the Ximenez region of Spain, and hand-bottled (hence the lack of anything so commercial as a label) by the seventh son of a seventh son of one of the MacCrimmons of Skye...

Or something like that.

Then pour two drams and, pausing only for some such appropriately ethnic valediction as *"Sliànte mhath, sliànte mhor"*• knock it back. To ensure success, instruct your victim to do so in one go, pressing the spirit against the hard palate with the tongue before letting it slide down the gullible gullet.

We guarantee this cannot fail; it renders the bluffee in no fit state to argue the matter.

* A lethally drinkable brew sold, in the interests of public order, in nip bottles.

• Pronounced 'Slarngy var, slarngy vor': Good health, great health!

# Regions

There are eight and a half distinct Scottish malt whisky regions, each producing whisky with its own distinctive sort of characteristic bluffery, viz:

## 1. Eastern

Occupying the seaboard of Aberdeenshire.

**Characteristics**: Bracing, keen, windswept, littoral.

**Typical malts**: *Glen Garioch*. Available at 15 and 21 years; claim to detect echoes of the herb garden in the aroma.

**Recommended malts**: *Lochnagar*, a rather stern and bracing malt with a hint of hairy knees; *Old Fettercairn*, light and fragrant, ideal for elevenses and much better for you than coffee; *Glenury Royal*, founded by the first man ever to walk 1,000 miles in 1,000 hours (in 1808), the distillery is now a housing estate: put a bottle of the 23-year-old on your Christmas wish-list.

## 2. Northern

i.e., north of Fort William but mostly north of Inverness.

**Characteristics**: Stern, muscular, uncompromising, hyperborean.

**Typical malts**: *Glenmorangie* (note that the accent

should be placed on the third syllable, even if it does sound odd), one of the Big names, light, smooth and refreshing and made in unusually tall pot-stills; *Tomatin*, a peaty malt that uses water drawn from a tributary of the River Findhorn.

**Recommended malts**: *Old Pulteney*, a Caithness malt said to have 'some of the strong characteristics of the northern temperament', but it might be a good idea not to say which characteristics these are; *Royal Brackla*, situated in Cawdor (where MacBeth got his first big break) and very hard to obtain; *Balblair* from a distillery which dates back to 1790 (or possibly 1749) and famous for its light, crumbly peat – so be sure to describe it as 'light-bodied and aromatic'.


## 3. Perthshire

A region which, for bluffing purposes, includes Loch Lomond.

**Characteristics**: Smooth, soft, comfortable, Georgic, effete.

**Typical malts**: *Blair Athol*, a principal ingredient of Bell's, which has a popular visitor centre.

**Recommended malts**: *Edradour*, a wholly delightful malt made with old-fashioned equipment in Scotland's smallest and prettiest distillery.

Insist this region is 'undervalued' – a useful phrase, since it leaves open the question of whether or not it deserves to be. *Glengoyne* can be described as 'a pleasant, unassuming little dram'; the malt is unpeated, and the distillery gets its water from a waterfall.

## 4. Lowland

**Characteristics**: Unassuming, disingenuous, unpretentious, self-effacing.

**Recommended malts**: Most Lowland malts are used for blending; enough said, maybe, except for *Littlemill* which is more than good enough to stand on its own though, alas, the distillery is now demolished. *Auchentoshan* is a Lowland malt made from Highland water, and the only one to be distilled three times; comment on its smoothness and 'Hibernian undertones'.

## 5. Island

Not including Islay, which is one, but including Oban, which is not.

**Characteristics**: Oceanic, temperamental, stoical, insular, or if you've had a few, 'ultimately thulian'.

**Typical malts**: *Highland Park*, an Orkney whisky (the most northerly in Britain); be sure to detect the burning of heather along with the seaweedy peat. The distillery was founded by Magnus Eunson, an illicit distiller who covered up his activities by being a Kirk elder and hiding barrels under the pulpit. It was built, somewhat foolishly, on a hill, so water has to be pumped up to it. It is knowing this sort of thing that makes you sound authoritative.

Drinking *Talisker*, the product of Skye's only distillery, may be compared with swallowing a Mahler symphony.

**Recommended malts**: *Scapa*, Orkney's other whisky, gains in bladder-wrack what it loses in heather; and *Isle of Jura* which 'combines the qualities of Islay malts minus the iodine, and West Highland malts minus the lingering sweetness'. Nonsense like this is essential to the really effective whisky bluff.

## 6. Islay

**Characteristics**: Penetrating, mordant, heroic, brackish.

**Typical malts**: *Laphroaig* (pronounced 'lafroyg'), best described as 'an acquired taste' and definitely a Big Whisky, the sort that lets you know you've had one. Tends to be monopolised by the plus-fours-brigade and suffers from over-reverential hype to the extent that it's in danger of becoming ascetic.

*Lagavulin* is made next door to *Laphroaig*, a situation neither relishes. It's a less heroic whisky, but arguably more user-friendly. *Bowmore* kindly donates its waste heat to warm the water in the local swimming pool. *Bruichladdich* (pronounced 'broo-ich-laddie') is Scotland's most westerly distillery though, alas, currently mothballed, and produces a warm, golden whisky that is astonishingly easy to drink.

**Recommended malts**: *Ardbeg*, closed during much of the 1980s owing to one of Britain's periodic out-breaks of economic recovery, but now back in business to celebrate the millennium; *Bunnahabhainn* ('boon-a-harven') has a much less peaty-seaweedy flavour than most Islay malts, and a good deal of it ends up in *Famous Grouse*.

*Caol lla* ('cole-eeler') is probably the most mentionable, being almost unheard-of and hard to get (unless you live in Italy or Venezuela); it has a singed wickerwork flavour, which you can ascribe to the original moisture of the malted barley being 2% rather than the usual 3%. This has probably got nothing to do with it, but that is beside the point.

## 7. Campbeltown

Of the twenty-odd Campbeltown malts of yore, only two remain in production, a situation you will deplore, of course.

**Characteristics**: Inimitable, enigmatic, ineffable.

**Recommended malts**: Both of them. *Glen Scotia* can be described as 'robust' and praised (or blamed) for its **guff** (see Glossary); the distillery is haunted by the shade of its 19th-century owner, who drowned himself after being tricked out of his savings on a sea cruise.

*Springbank* is one of the few private operations still in the hands of the family who founded it (in 1828) and one of only two (the other is *Glenfiddich*) where everything, including bottling, is done on the premises: this ought to predispose sentimentalists to approve the product. Look out for the *'West Highland Malt'* bottling of the 1966 vintage, made with locally-grown barley.

## 8. Speyside

There are dozens of Speyside distilleries, mostly clustered about a line from Elgin to Dufftown. Be sure to quote the old Speyside jingle: 'Rome was built on seven hills, Dufftown stands on seven stills'.

The fame of all Speyside whiskies rests on the water, but hardly any distilleries actually draw theirs from the Spey itself. This is what experts call a 'phenomenological oxymoron', and the rest of us call a flat contradiction.

**Characteristics**: Pure, scarifying, ethereal, spiritual, rounded, Grampian.

**Typical malts**: Two of the Big Whiskies are here:

1) *Glenfiddich*
2) *The Macallan*.

There is not much bluffing to be done with these so you should say that, "On the whole, they deserve their reputation." This sounds as though you have done a lot of comparative research and are not the sort to be taken in by general opinion. Suggest that *Cardhu* and *Linkwood* "deserve to be much better known".

**Recommended malts**: The ones of which little is heard, for example:

*Convalmore* a defunct distillery whose product is available once in a blue moon,
*Glendullan* a favourite tipple of Edward VII,
*Glenallachie* now used only for blending,
*Knockando* (pronounced 'croch-an-doo'), the only whisky to give the dates of both distilling and

bottling on the label, so you can sound excessively knowledgeable if you decant it first,

*Mortlach* full-bodied but light on the peat, and a connoisseur's favourite.

The town of **Elgin** in this region is bluffing material on two counts:

a) It's the home of *Linkwood*, whose one-time manager (a Mr. Roderick MacKenzie) forbade the removal of spiders' webs from the stillroom in the belief that they contributed to the quality of the product.
b) It's the home of **Gordon & MacPhail**, whose shop in South Street is a Mecca for fundamentalists. As well as stocking dozens of otherwise barely obtainable single malts under their 'Connoisseur's Choice' label, they also have a sample of *Mortlach* dating from the brief accession of Edward VIII and some 25-year-old *Glenlivet* distilled during the Battle of Britain. On no account attempt to bluff your way in this hallowed sanctum; even venturing a mild opinion is only recommended for the brave. It might be wiser just to pretend that you've been there.

## 8½. Glenlivet

**Characteristics**: Unmistakable.

Glenlivet is an essential but dangerous bluffing zone: essential, because it is where most of the best malts come from (or claim to come from), dangerous because it tends to be inhabited by the most ferocious sort of dedicated whisky drinker, who might just know more than you are pretending to. This will not do, and the only proof against it is a crash course in:

# Glenlivetology

All you really need to know is that Glenlivet is in Speyside (top of the sticking-out bit on the right-hand side of Scotland), location of 57 malt whisky distilleries for reasons that are mostly to do with water and history. To this valley came a refugee from the lost Jacobite cause; his name was Gow – which is from the Gaelic word for a smith – so, in order to out-wit the pursuing Hanoverians, he cleverly changed his name to Smith.

Smith (whose initial was J) set up a distillery and passed it on to his son and grandson, who carried on making Glenlivet whisky in the traditional way, in other words, without paying tax. George IV, on a visit to Scotland in 1822, claimed he drank nothing else but illegal *Glenlivet*. This made things even more romantic, not to mention profitable.

The grandson (G) eventually bought a licence from the government so as to make whisky without all the excitement of dawn raids, midnight keg-laden flits through the heather hotly pursued by redcoats, and so on. Two other distillers soon followed his example. Their former colleagues took a dim view of this and threatened to burn down the three distilleries with their turncoat occupants inside them. During this time Smith is reported to have 'slept with two hair-trigger pistols under his pillow'.

By the mid-19th century, G. Smith and his son (J.G.) had built a new, much bigger distillery and the Glenlivet name had become highly popular – so popular, in fact, that dozens of other distilleries (some of them 50 miles away) were using it. J.G. Smith went to court in 1871 and won (or, as some say, lost) a famous judgement, namely that:

a) Only his whisky could call itself 'The Glenlivet';

b) Others could, however, hyphenate their names with it.

This was very canny – a thing all Scots are supposed to be, when they are not being heroic. The firm of G & J.G. Smith is now a subsidiary of The Glenlivet and Glen Grant Distilleries Ltd., which is a subsidiary of The Glenlivet Distillers Ltd., which is a subsidiary of Seagram plc, one of the world's biggest multinationals – but even that hasn't ruined it.

You have no choice but to acknowledge that *G & J.G. Smith's Glenlivet* (*The Glenlivet*) is the best malt whisky there is, was, or ever will be; this is because (a) it probably is (was, etc.) and (b) it has a very lovely label. There can be no limit to your appreciation of the stuff, though this does not mean you have to like it. The true bluffer need not actually drink *Glenlivet* whisky at all – all he or she has to do is insist that the one required brand, the only one worth crossing the road for, isn't available. Short of inventing one (e.g., *Mitsubishi-Glenlivet)* we suggest *Pittyvaich* (virtually unobtainable) or *Glen Keith* (used for *Chivas Regal*, and vanishingly rare). There are 17 hyphenated Glenlivets altogether and so long as you steer clear of Elgin you're unlikely to find them all in one place.

Alternatively, you could point out that within a circle drawn to include all the distilleries which claim '*Glenlivet*' in their name there are 30-odd distilleries that do not, although they have as much right to do so as the ones who do. You may compare this with the Burgundy/Beaujolais debate.

Among the unhyphenated malt whiskies is *The*

*Macallan*, which shares with *Glenfiddich* the distinction of being a malt whisky most people have actually heard of. Observe that *The Macallan* is distilled by a company called Macallan-Glenlivet and indeed was, once upon a time, known as such. However there is no doubt that the prefix 'The' sounds classier. This sort of high-altitude snobbery is meat and drink to true believers.

Other well-known quasi-Glenlivets are *Aberlour, Dufftown, Glenfarclas, Glen Grant*, and *Tamdhu*. For bluffing purposes, however, we recommend a quasi-Glenlivet non-Glenlivet, and the best of these is a malt called *Dallas Mhor*; a good choice because it is:

a) distilled in the Glenlivet area (give or take a bit);
b) a rather odd name;
c) pretty well unheard of, and
d) not made any more.*

Nearly all blends, however inexpensive, contain trace elements of *The Glenlivet* and however downmarket you go, the chances are that you will find a smidgin of a Glenlivet somewhere. Claim to be able to recognise its 'unique Speyside characteristics'. If challenged to describe what these are, say: "Quite different from those of any other region. Absolutely distinctive. Utterly unique." This sort of appreciative gobbledegook usually goes down a treat with professional whisky drinkers. It seems to mean something to them. Perhaps, secretly, they all have to buy the cut-price kind, too.

* Unavailable whisky is a good bluffer's ploy, as in "Of course, if you *really* want to taste a good whisky..."

# WHISKY NOTES

## Labels

Labels, especially those on blended whiskies, give very little away and should be admired for their artistry rather than read for their information. Remember that only whisky distilled (and, preferably, blended though not necessarily bottled) in Scotland is allowed to call itself 'Scotch whisky' and that anything purporting to be a single malt should state the name of the distillery whence it came. Any malt that does not is probably a vatted one. Look for the capacity (75cl on an ordinary bottle) and alcoholic strength (at least 70° or 40% by volume).

Note that words like *Special, Finest, Extra, Old, Auld, Reserve, Supreme, Cream, Ancient, Matured*, and so on, though quite possibly reassuring (like the old claim of Carnation milk to come from contented cows), are completely meaningless.

First prize for appealing labelling probably ought to go to Hedges & Butler, specialists in the aristocratic end of the blended market, whose brands are (in ascending order of pomp and price): *Royal, Royal Special De Luxe, Royal Finest De Luxe, Royal Supreme De Luxe* and *Royal Imperial De Luxe*. This rather suggests that 'finest' and 'supreme' are not intended to be taken too seriously; 'special' by this token means 'relatively ordinary'.

A close runner-up is Dewar's, whose posh blend goes under the name of *Dewar's De Luxe Ancestor*; people with ordinary, run-of-the-mill pedigrees probably ought to leave it alone. You can safely describe *Dewar's Ne Plus Ultra* as 'unique' without even tasting it. Note that the ordinary blend is referred to as

'White Label' in Britain and 'Dooers' in the United States.

*Vat 69* got its name as a result of a blind tasting session of a number of vats of experimental blended whiskies, or so the story goes. You might speculate aloud as to what sort of state the tasters' palates were in after sampling the other 68.

*Famous Grouse* is known simply as 'Grouse' among the cognoscenti, who naturally despise anyone foolish enough to be taken in by a self-fulfilling marketing ploy like the use of the word 'famous' on a label. It is valued by real drinkers for its superior malty flavour despite its higher-than-average price, and is popular with ordinary mortals for precisely the opposite reason.

Be somewhat contemptuous of anyone who buys one of the brands sold in pseudo-authentic stone flagons; *Usquebach* is one such, a toe-curling misspelling of the Gaelic. Another is *Ye Whisky of Ye Monks*, a de luxe blend which sounds as if it has been distilled, blended and bottled in a theme park.

For dedicated label-bluffers we recommend two blends in particular:

*Te Bheag nan Eilean* (pronounced 'tchay vek nan yellan') – the sole blend of a company based on the tiny Isle Ornsay (or Eilean Iarmain) off the south coast of Skye and run by a reformed merchant banker with a passion for Gaelic and fancy whisky labels. It contains a pleasingly high proportion of 5-12 year-old Speyside malts, so be sure to taste, name and date a few of them. No-one will be able to prove you wrong.

*Uam Var* – a blended whisky produced by the makers of *Drambuie*.

The only really safe ploy – since you can pretty well make it up as you go along with the help of as many bluffing elements as you can muster all at one go – is to declare that you are only interested in the quality and provenance of the contents, rather than such artifices as baroque labels, ribbons, blobs of wax, or dangly ornaments round the neck of the bottle.

# Mixers

Mixers ought generally to be deprecated outside the privacy of your own drinks cupboard. Reserve your most withering scorn for soda, but note in passing that some of the more eccentric concoctions (e.g., whisky-and-Lucozade) were invented in the sweet-toothed West Highlands. An old Gaelic proverb has it that 'There are two things best taken naked, and one of them is whisky' and to maintain your status as an expert you will say that only two mixers are allowed:

1. Water, preferably from a Highland tap or a bottle; or
2. More whisky.

# Glasses

Whisky should be drunk from a cylindrical glass, preferably cut-crystal with a design that reaches at least one-third of the way up (so you know how much whisky to put in) and a heavy bottom (to make that satisfying clunk when you put it down). Avoid the hip flask unless you fill it with economy blend; your body heat, and the reaction of the spirit with the metal, will then obscure the rebarbative flavour. Malt in a tulip glass is recommended, but anyone who serves you malt whisky in a brandy balloon is rather more deserving of pity than contempt.

# 'Scotch': A Warning

Scotch Whisky is defined in European Community legislation as (among other things) 'Whisky which has been distilled in Scotland'. This gives due recognition to the unique qualities of Scottish water, air, peat, climate, industrial relations and so on.

There are two things to avoid, however, viz:

1. Calling Scotch whisky 'Scotch', which is considered vulgar.
2. Calling malt whisky 'Scotch whisky', which is not merely vulgar but also wrong, since the law allows Scotch whisky to be distilled from various cereals as well as barley.

Refer any disbeliever to the report of the 1908 Royal Commission – 'Whisky is a spirit obtained by distillation from a mash of cereal grains saccharified by the diastase of malt' – and point out that only the peculiar genius of the great and the good could make such a nobly enjoyable thing as whisky sound so horribly unattractive.

Amaze your audience by remarking that the value of whisky currently maturing in casks in Scotland far exceeds that of all the Bank of England's gold reserves.

"It makes you think," you murmur. Then quote Rabelais: "When I drink, I think: and when I think, I drink" and hold your glass out.

# GLOSSARY

## The Process

The making of malt whisky employs a sumptuous vocabulary, something like a cross between a sex manual and a handbook of Masonic ritual. Short of wading through various worthy tomes on the subject (a thing no self-respecting bluffer would ever do) your only other hope of becoming fluent in whiskybabble is to join a conducted tour of a distillery. This has one big advantage – you get a free dram at the end of it (not at the beginning, too many people would escape) and two big disadvantages:

1. If the distillery is in operation you cannot hear what is being explained to you and the staff all have better things to do, e.g., malting, grinding, sparging, mashing, brewing, stilling, rummaging, not to mention waiting for the foreshot.

2. If the distillery is not in operation because you are visiting during the 'silent season' (July-September) you can hear all right but you might as well have stayed at home because there is nothing going on to look at, and the staff are all busy gardening.

Either way it is a bit too much like hard work. Much better to pour yourself a fat dram, put your feet up, and let us take the tour for you, thus:

**Rough dressing** – The removal from barley of odd bits of stalk, fieldmouse and fertiliser bag that might have sneaked in.

**Malting** – Germination of damp barley to turn it into malt; regularly raked and turned to prevent its sproutlets becoming entangled.

**Kilning** – Part-roasting of germinated barley grains over a peat furnace in line with the Highland Heritage (Marketing) Act, the Euro-Peat Directive (number 2746/xviii/D) and the Scottish Tourist Board's Ethnic Aroma Initiative.

**Grist** – The little-known origin of the well-known expression, 'grist to the mill' and what whole grain is ground down into before being used for brewing and distilling, or wasted on luxuries like bread.

**Tun room** – The first (or, in the US, second) floor of a distillery, containing a number of huge vessels whose bottoms are located on the floor below.

**Sparging** – Exciting word for the otherwise fairly tedious business of pouring very hot (but not boiling) water over malt grist.

**Mash tun** – Sort of giant Ascot boiler used for sparging.

**Mashing** – What goes on in the mash tun, after sparging; think of 'mash' as in tea, rather than potatoes.

**Balfour-Schock-Gusmer Lauteran** – Fine old Highland name for a white-hot technological, fifth-generation sort of mash tun which may (or may not) contribute to the distinctive flavour of *Tomatin* single malt.

**Extraction waters** – Queasily obstetric term for the warm, brown, sticky fluid that is run off from the bottom of the mash tun and then fermented. This happens twice, usually; the third and fourth lots are heated up again – be sure to say 'recycled' – for the next lot of sparging.

**Draff** – Soggy leftovers of malted barley grist after extraction of the above. Used as cattle-feed.

**Worts** – What extraction waters turn into during their journey from the mash tun to the:

**Wash back** – Gargantuan wooden vessel used for fermenting the sugary worts by adding shovelfuls of ravenous yeast and standing well clear.

**Wash** – What worts turn into after fermentation: a thin, dreary, grizzling sort of sour ale, not entirely unlike low alcohol lager.

**Alcohols** – Always plural, note: wash contains a large number of higher and lower alcohols, including ethanol. Remember that it's always better to be thought of as an ethanolophile than spoken of as an alcoholic.

**Carbon dioxide** – The other product of fermentation. Note that the Loch Lomond distillery captures it, compresses it, and sells it to be turned into the various sorts of fizzy stuff you're not allowed to put in malt whisky.

**Stillroom** – Situated on the ground (or, in the US, first) floor. Alchemical laboratory, destination of the wash; inhabited by **stillmen**, the aristocracy of the distillery workforce (dent-maintenance operatives, foreshot-watchers, fusel-detectors, men in white coats with Parker pens in their top pockets, etc).

**Pot-still** – Nuptial chamber of the Chymical Wedding; atavistic union of ying and yang, animus and anima; the large copper retort for the heating, separation, evaporation and recondensation of various alcohols present in lightly fermented malty water.

**Worm** – Apt name for the long, thin, coiled-up wiggly tube that comes out of the top of a still and is used for recondensing evaporated alcohols; you can't see it because it's hidden in a large tank of cold water.

**Low wines** – Product of the first distillation and quite undrinkable, even with the addition of 7-Up and a couple of cocktail umbrellas.

**Pot ale** – Residue of first distillation; fed to cattle with advanced D.D.S. (see page 6), who no longer get a decent buzz from draff.

**Reflux** – In humans, the unpleasant result of having a weak œsophagal sphincter; in distilling, the pleasant result of encouraging the heavier volatile vapours to fall back into the still instead of passing out into the spirit.

**Spent lees** – Residue of the second distillation, and practically the only by-product that is poured down the drain; being terribly organic, it's obviously very good for something-or-other. Killer algae, probably.

**Spirit still** – The end of the line; destination of the low wines.

**Spirit safe** – Ornately padlocked fishtank through which pass various end products of the spirit still, viz:

**Foreshot** – Name for all the volatile, flighty alcohols that aren't wanted in whisky. Modern distilleries test for it with state-of-the-art technology (e.g., the Sykes hydrometer, invented in 1818). You should claim to know of one where they still use the much more romantic method of watching it turn a glass of water milky-blue.

**Middle cut** – This is *it*, the liquid that will be whisky one day. It accounts for approximately 40% of the total output of the spirit still; exactly how much varies from one distillery to another and is, of course, a secret.

**Feints** – The last lot of alcohols to come off, be saved, and added to the next lot of low wines to be distilled. Also known as **aftershot**; use whichever word appeals to you more, according to the company you're in and the circumstances under which you're in it.

**Fusel oil** – A heavy alcohol present in the feints, some of which is required in the middle cut in order to give the whisky flavour; it is an essential constituent of **cling** and a contributor to **guff** (see under Taste in Product Glossary that follows) and can be held responsible for any ill effects.

**White spirit** – Not the stuff with which you clean paintbrushes but freshly distilled, 120° proof liquor unsullied by water and unadulterated by charcoal, pajarette, caramel, etc. One whiff is usually enough to cauterise the nasal tissue; drinking it may be likened to being hit over the head with a ten-ton bunch of freesias. Claim to like it.

**Maturing** – a) Process you have undergone in order to become a whisky bluffer; b) Process whisky has undergone in oak casks, usually **butts** (108 gallons) or **hogsheads** (55 gallons), for a minimum of three years in a bonded warehouse.

**Cutting** – Regrettable practice of diluting white spirit with water before maturing; repeated with mature whisky before bottling.

**Proof** – a) Action of testing your hypothesis by opening someone else's bottle; b) Fiendishly complicated measurement of alcoholic strength, designed to bamboozle people who are not fazed by percentages. Originally this had something to do with the flashpoint of gunpowder: if your gun did not go off, it meant they were watering the whisky. Spirit that is 100° proof is 57.1% alcohol and 42.9% water. All you need to remember is that 70° proof = 40% alcohol. (In America, where they have smaller gallons and more volatile gunpowder, this re-translates as 80° proof.)

# The Product

As it is advisable to be familiar with a selection of terms to employ when confronted with the spirit itself we offer the following, together with their simple definitions.

For the true whisky buff, a single well-chosen word is all that suffices, but be sure to say it with quivering emotion, and with a fanatical gleam in at least one eye.

## Appearance

**Golden** – Anything lighter than amber.

**Citrine** – Too pale to be golden.

**Amber** – Too dark to be citrine.

**Fulvous** – Reserve for one which cannot be called brown (because it would be demeaning) or tawny (because port got in first).

**Pellucid** – Use instead of 'clear' when what you see through the glass is particularly worth looking at.

**Lambent** – Seems to glow with an inner light.

**Limpid** – Seductively lambent; only a fool could resist.

**Incandescent** – Looks as if you've set fire to it.

**Polished** – Served in a clean glass.

**Serene** – Hasn't been served with a fizzy mixer.

**Plangent** – Cries out to be swallowed.

**Rich** – You've seen the price on the bottle.

**Cling** – The snail-trails on the inside of the glass after you've tilted it. An absence of cling means you're about to drink a blended whisky with very little malt in it: prepare to be disparaging. Cling is caused by the essential fusel oils in malt whisky, so its presence is highly encouraging.

## Nose

**Brisk** or **ardent** – One which makes your eyes water.

**Dominant** – You've stuck your nose in too far.

**Delicate** – It doesn't make you squint.

**Discreet** – It probably isn't whisky.

**Insistent** – It follows you round the room.

**Bite** – Just as effective as Vick's vapour rub in clearing your sinuses.

**Aromatic** – It smells of something other than whisky.

**Pungent** – Smells strongly of whisky.

**Fragrant** – The sophisticates' word for 'nice'.

**Elusive** or **fugitive** – The ideal non-committal comment.

**Finish** – That which you go on tasting long after your glass is empty. Very much a personal experience, it can be described with whatever adjectival inspiration comes to mind. The last thing that comes to mind before sleep or real life takes over and spoils it all is known as 'the **'tail'** – as in: "Hmmm... a brisk, heathery finish with a hint of crushed bracken on the tail."

## Taste

**Insistent** – No good sucking a mint afterwards.

**Lingering** – No good trying Listerine either.

**Haunting** – Stays with you longer than you expect, or perhaps, wish.

**Astringent** – Makes you worry about your tooth enamel.

**Penetrating** – You've just lost your tooth enamel, gums and soft palate.

**Assertive** – Not awfully nice, frankly.

**Peaty** – A blend of garden bonfire and Dutch pipe tobacco.

**Heathery** – Not quite peaty.

**Nutty** – Two of these will do instead of lunch.

**Littoral** – A little reminiscent of seaweed with a hint of Loch Fyne kipper.

**Sanative** – A bit like TCP.

**Mellow** – You catch yourself beginning to believe in the United Nations, and weather forecasts.

**Bracing** – Like getting out of bed on a Hebridean autumn morning.

**Light** – Suitable for breakfast.

**Smooth** – Doesn't leave you gasping for air.

**Creamy** – Clogs the tongue.

**Suave** – Bland.

**Guff** – The stuff which makes you go red in the face and start clutching your uvula; blame insufficient maturing and/or too much fusel oil.

**Distinctive** – Definitely some sort of whisky. A word that elegantly conceals your inability to say anything useful.

**Mighty** – You happen to know it's something famous like *Laphroaig*, *The Macallan* or *Smith's Glenlivet*. Most of the above rolled into one.

NB: Claim to detect any or all of these 'Nose' and 'Taste' qualities in the 'Tail' and the 'Finish'.

# Character

A combination of appearance, nose and taste with other factors thrown in, such as history, reputation, bottle shape, design of label, price, etc.

**Heroic** – Probably a little overrated but you wouldn't fancy picking a quarrel with it.

**Noble** – Can be used of any whisky which does not make you cough, choke, cry, pick arguments with strangers or feel remorseful the following morning. Use especially for whiskies you feel deserve to be better-known than they are, like *Clynelish, Linkwood, Glengarrioch, Bruichladdich, Talisker, King Henry VIII* 12-year-old.

**Rounded** – Interesting bottle; elegant label; smells fine; tastes nice; does not give you heartburn; useful change from £30.

**Affected** – Any whisky promoted for its snob-value with advertisements of the only-a-few-of-you-can-afford-me variety.

**Austere** – Sort of whisky that can only be appreciated after a lifetime's devotion. There are, as it happens, better things to do with a lifetime.

**Ascetic** – Appealing to all the senses except those of taste and smell.

**Numinous** – After two glasses you decide to teach yourself Gaelic.

**Generous** – The ultimate accolade; to be used of whiskies which, to quote famous former excise officer turned writer Neil Gunn: '... recall the world of hills and glens, of raging elements, of shelter, of divine ease ...'

Note that a glass or two of a really generous whisky would enable you to recall bens, glens, etc., even if you had lived all your life in Snake Pit, Arizona. Alternatively, apply the term to any whisky served by an open-handed host and, if it brings out the same qualities in you, feel free to call it 'noble' as well. Have another one, why not. Oh, and you might as well make that a double.

# THE AUTHOR

For fifteen years Sussex-born David Milsted lived in the Scottish islands of Orkney (*Highland Park* and *Scapa*), Islay (*Ardbeg, Lagavulin, Laphroaig, Bowmore, Bruichladdich, Bunnahabhainn* and *Caol Ila*) and Skye (*Talisker*), which is as near to heaven as any whisky fancier could get. He claims that he would choose to work in a distillery if he ever had to get a proper job – which, fortunately, he hasn't.

A professional author, his greatest pleasure besides writing is organising whisky tastings. He moved back to England on a mission to cure his fellow-countrymen from Distillate Deficiency Syndrome, and now does so from Dorset.

---

**Further titles in the Bluffer's® Guide series:**

Accountancy, Archaeology, Astrology & Fortune Telling, Ballet, Chess, The Classics, Computers, Consultancy, Cricket, Doctoring, Economics, The Flight Deck, Football, Golf, The Internet, Jazz, Law, Management, Marketing, Men, Men & Women, Middle Age, Music, Opera, Philosophy, Psychology, Public Speaking, The Quantum Universe, Relationships, The Rock Business, Rugby, Science, Seduction, Sex, Skiing, Small Business, Stocks & Shares, Tax, Teaching, University, Wine, Women.

**www.bluffers.com**